Marriage on Fire

Journeying from Ceremony to Matrimony

A 30 Day

Marriage Devotional Guide

DWIGHT & DEIDRA ROUSSAW

Marriage on Fire: Journeying from Ceremony to Matrimony

A 30-Day Marriage Devotional Guide

Copyright © 2016 Dwight and Deidra Roussaw

ISBN: 1-943833-09-5
ISBN-13: 1-943833-09-5

PUBLISHED BY:
KPLA PUBLISHING LLC
P.O. BOX 9819
HAMPTON, VA 23670
WWW.KPLAPUBLISHING.COM

FOREWORD

Ministers Dwight and Deidra Roussaw are both very much loved and respected nationally and internationally for their vibrant commitment to helping married couples maximize their marital success. Their unswerving loyalty to strengthening marital unions over the years has yielded them a widespread global marriage ministry. Simply put, Dwight and Deidra want to see couples fulfill their marital vows, accomplish their daily marital goals and live out their ultimate marital dreams! To that end, they continued to facilitate and encourage marital enrichment thru marriage conferences, cruises, gatherings, counseling and coaching, to name a few.

Their most recent effort to reach and empower married couples is contained in this "30-Days Of Marriage Devotional Guide." It is a well written devotional designed to guide and encourage couples on a daily basis thru 30-day cycles of mental, spiritual and physical renewal. Their system of applying relevant bible passages to the daily life struggles common to married couples becomes an important tool for successful marriage renewal, improvement and family building.

Dwight and Deidra take the readers on an exciting day by day journey through brief but powerful devotional discussions of important marital issues and topics such as: marital passion and communication, tone of speech, mutual love and respect, money matters, sexual purity, pleasure and power, parenting, promises and gratitude, to name a few. So, beloved, we recommend you take that first step, turn that first page and move into your 30 day devotional pattern before God and with your spouse.

Dr. S. Todd Townsend and Dr. Cleo V. Townsend

DEDICATION

This book is dedicated to the families across the universe for effective and good communication between them and God.

Happy reading.

.

CONTENTS

ACKNOWLEDGMENTS

First and foremost we give honor to whom honor is due and that's our Lord and Savior Jesus who is the Christ. Special thanks to my mom, the late Carrie M. Camp. My mom was a great asset to whom I've become, her wisdom and knowledge has set me on the correct path. She was full of integrity if she loved you, you knew it yet if she didn't care for you, you knew that as well. My mom was Mantua's favorite mom, she helped everyone in the community and her children never lacked anything. My dad the late Robert Clark, was a man of a few words but he meant what he said. He had that personality trait which made him everyone's favorite.

I'd like to thank my only child, Little Carrie. My daughter is such an amazing person; she has a big personality and has always been very encouraging. I'd like to thank my grandchildren Kairi, Kayla, Kaleb, Kahle and my grand angel Kristian. These little people bring so much joy into my life, they are a part of my encouragement team, they are very loving and caring.

My siblings Darryl, Russell, Flo, Pam, Reggie, Bobby, Pearl, Nicole and the late Gary and Michael. My siblings are some awesome and amazing people, they made sure my little sister and I had all of our wants while being reared. They protected and provided alongside my mom, they really spoiled us and I appreciate the love they've always demonstrated.

Thanks to my Aunt Doris who always had a pleasant posture and reaches out to check on the family at all times, I truly appreciate her.

To my mother Diane Gibson whom I am well pleased with, for God has chosen you to give birth unto me. Your life teaching experiences, sacrifices, motherly love and prayers has help groom me from childhood to adulthood. I love you!

To my grandparents, the late Routha and Mary Roussaw, your marriage of over 50 years became the living model and standard for me. My sisters, Mary and Diane and late brother Shawn, growing up with you was amazing and I thank you for allowing me to represent what a big brother is to his younger siblings. My cousin Martina, thank you for your years of support and being a true friend to my wife. To my best man Haisonn Shadding. Wow! So much could be said of who you are and how much you mean to the Roussaw family but I must keep it brief. You are the essence of a friend but closer to than a brother. Your willingness to put others before yourself is far greater than most. I thank you for trusting and walking beside me through my good, bad and ugly. Love you Bro! To my good thing Deidra Renee Roussaw, Oh' how beautiful and awesome you are. You have provided friendship, motivation, support, commitment, dedication, patience, love, and prayers for me which has made our marriage journey Twogether worth living. I thank you and love you with an unspeakable joy!

Many Thanks to our pastors Dr. S. Todd and Dr. Cleo V. Townsend; they are both the best bishop and pastor a person could ask for. They are our friends, leaders, our travel partners & sister and brother for over 25 years. Thanks to our mentors, Pastor Emanuel and Lady Martina Lambert, they have sown seeds into our lives as well as our daughter. They are our daughter's God-Parents and they are some exceptional God parents, they poured so much into our marriage, they went above and beyond to make sure we both succeeded. We wholeheartedly love and appreciate them. Thanks to Mom Darlene Townsend Henderson, she has always been able to offer a resolution for any situation; she's one of a kind. Thanks to our friends Attorney J. Gregory and Dr. Chevelta Smith, these pastors have helped us reach out to married couples in a tangible way. Their desire to see marriages flourish is priceless and we adore them and their children.

We appreciate our TWOgether Marriages team (Avery & Ciara, Will & Eve, Clinton & Stacy, Fred & Gwen, Keith & Nicole, Henry & Crystal, Fred & Tina, Phil & Nieda, Richard & Nephetina, Orlando & Tinesha and Will & Shanna) Our 2. Be One Marriage Fellowship Leadership team & family, we can't express the appreciation you all have demonstrated towards the Body of Christ, you are some wonderful leaders (Michael & Jocelyn, Mark & Debra, Devin & Tara, Victor & Felicia and Darin & Fern) Thanks for your diligence towards the married couples at The Resurrection Center and beyond. Thanks to our Eusebia family, Dr. Harold & Dalia Arnold and Gene & Marsha Redd have gathered marriage leaders from around the nation to sphere head a relentless task that caters to married couples, we're honored to serve alongside them on the marriage battlefield. Thanks to the late Dr. Myles Munroe for empowering us with tools and knowledge on the annual Tropical Leadership Retreat in Nassau, Bahamas. It was a blessing to have spent some quality time with such an awesome leader for him to impart so valuable nuggets into our marriage.

Thanks to Dr. Stacia and Arianna Pierce, they are the best success coaches; their dedicated leadership skills are greatly appreciated. Dr. Stacia please enjoy our hero project, we're honored to be a part of your coaching team. Our nephews and nieces, Brother Chris & Sister Carin Johnson & Minister Al & Kristina Motley, we're Godly proud of the dedication you've put into your marriages as the younger generation you all are setting trends. We love you!

Our good friends who we love dearly: Elders Larry & Nadira Alston, Henry & Simone Collins, Pastor Keon & Rev. Tamika Gerow, Pastor Warren & Lady Cynthia McKnight, Bob & Erica colbert, Vincent & Tomorrow Jenkins, Derek & Tia Stanford, Greg & Brianna Downing, Greg & Lani Glasco, Pastor Marcos & Lady Amarillis Mercado, Ministers Rhonda & Roger Dickson, Ministers Donald & Precious Graham, Chefs Matthew & Sharon Pierce, Rodney & Liz Banks, Broch & Daveena Clinton, Tyrone & Diana Hill, Chris & Eboni Fountain, Brian & Kimrenee Patterson, Tyrone & Latanya Jenifer, Carey & Kendra Haynes, Dyon & Jackie Scott, Pastor Anthony & Lady Adrianne McKenzie, Kenny & Sheila Barnhill, BJ & Kayla Johnson, Al & Josie Russell, Fred & Bonnie Moon, Brian & Celeste Payne, Clayton & Cheriss Beale, James & Cynthia Greene, Tony & Daphne Oliver, Donald & Lynette Smith, Wendell & Doreen Shockley, Peter & Eartha Mack, Fred & Sophia Dean, Gary& Lynette Wall, Chris & Da-Nay Macklin, Chris & Felicia Houston, Donald & Adrienne Relli, Oscar & Sharon Sadler, Darryl & Jerri Riley, John & Donna Greene, Juan & Kayla Baxter, Elder Keith & Michelle Beckett, Leroy & Marlene Payton, Mark & Christine Bell, Luther & Dorothy Robinson, Elders Thom & Marilyn Gwaltney, Matthew & Aliya Covington, Marquest & Murlene Clark, Damond & Nicole Young, Byron & Nikita Jackson, Omar & Rosita Chatt , Pastor Al & Lady Pam Gibson, Benny & Pat Daniels, Pernell & Lorie Forrester, Tyrone & Quiana Smack, Minister Martin & Rhonda Boyd, Rick & Kim Taylor, Kevin & Stephanie Tarkenton, Kenny & Tiffany Rouse, Bob & Tonya Thorpe, Doug & Earline Reed, Mark & Fatimah Knight, Bill & Cassandra Mabrey, Donald & Valerie Simms, Victor & Vivian Strong, and Mike & Millie Santiago.

And special thanks to the best Sandals & Beaches Business Development Manager David Ridge, for always assisting us with creating a unique experience for married couples during our annual Marriage on Fire Retreats.

$\mathcal{D}ay\ 1$

KEEP THE FIRE BURNING

"And above all things, have fervent charity among yourselves:
for charity shall cover the multitude of sins"
1 Peter 4: 8

On a few occasions, we have been able to stumble on gatherings of married couples in estranged relationships with their spouses, and on each of these occasions, we have made sure to sit and listen so we can pick useful knowledge from their rantings. Commonly, from what we fathom, the major problem that can be held responsible for most of the discord is "Dead Sparkle".

The scripture says in 2 Corinthians 2:11 "Lest the devil get an advantage of us, for we are not ignorant of his devices". As Christians, we are expected to have a better understanding of what God teaches, and his directions on every ramification of a Christian's life including love, which is the greatest of his teachings. It is foolhardy, for one to allow the flame of love die in marriage.

Usually, the courtship years are full of fun and intrigue and sparkle, and then, more often than not, after marriage, a nonchalance washes over both parties. The sweet little gestures, the kind words, the surprises, the date nights, the lovely expressions of loves through written words amongst other things are discontinued. These same things are the players that kept the fire of love burning blue during courtship.

Spouses seem to be overwhelmed by chores, their jobs, finances, children, and a host of other things, hence losing sight of the truly important things. As said earlier in the scripture referred to (2 Corinthians 2:11). This neglect of duties towards the emotions of one another, and resultant distance between both hearts lead to an unavoidable friction from which couples may never recover.

A lot of our problems sometimes are not entirely spiritual, but stem from basic things right before our eyes that we fail to pay attention to. Therefore, in accordance with the directive of the main scripture, revive the gestures and courtesies of courtship in your marriages. Don't lose the sense of responsibilities to the sense of possession that tying the knot gives you. It may lead you to take each other for granted, which in the long run results in discord. Keep at the back of your mind, that a feeling is as useless as inexistent if it is not expressed, just as good intentions don't hold water till they are put into actions.

So, yes, you love your spouse, and they know, but doubts will set in if you don't show them you love them with actions. Your love can only grow if you keep showing it and expressing it to one another. Make it a conscious duty to re-ignite the enthusiasm of the courtship days. Try new things twogether, communicate thoroughly, study the word of God twogether to be on the same page in your spirituality - mark the word "TWOGETHER", as you're one and must do things as such.

If we do these things and more, we might just be able to save our marriage from hitting the rocks, and falling victim to the devices of the devil.

PRAYER POINTS:

- Thank God for the new day, and new opportunity.

- In your own words, and as directed by the spirit after reading today's devotional, hold hands with your spouse and ask the almighty God for the grace to continue showing love to one another in ways that will strengthen your union.

Day 2

ANGER MANAGEMENT

"'Be ye kind one to another, tenderhearted, forgiving one another, even as God for Christ's sake hath forgiven you."
Ephesians 4:32

We were watching the news one evening, and there was this young man being paraded for smashing his fiancé's head against the bathroom wall. The young man couldn't manage to say anything when he was asked to explain how it happened. All he did was cry, and shake his head, and cry some more. From what we sensed, he regretted what he'd done, and couldn't even come to grips with the reality of his situation - he had taken the life of his fiancé. We couldn't keep watching the entire incident; therefore we turned the television off.

For weeks after, the scenario kept playing in our minds, causing us unexplainable sadness each time. Here's the truth about the matter. No sane human will willingly take the life of another, let alone a loved one who is dear to their heart.

Can two people communicate without having disagreements at some point? I think not. Marriage is a union or coming twogether of TWO different people from different backgrounds, with different views, opinions, desires, approaches to life, ways of doing things - the list is endless - who come twogether to be ONE. Bless God for the gospel and it's teachings, it shows us how to live peacefully twogether as one under the guidance of the most high.

This said, we cannot entirely rule out our personal differences. This is where love comes to play - our constant endeavor to bridge the gap between our differences and learning to tolerate each other's excesses in love. As Christians, we are different from the rest of the world, and therefore should do things differently. It is imperative that we allow the spirit of God take charge in times when anger, misunderstandings, and misgivings are in play. Especially so we don't utter damaging words that can't be taken back.

The flesh is always eager to take control of our minds and actions, and if we allow it, we will end up doing or saying things that we may never be able to correct or come back from. It is human to be angry, but whether or not we allow our anger to get the best of us is the true test of our love, and of course our Christ-like life.

The young man who took his fiancé's life by smashing her head into a wall may have not thought of such an outcome, but his failure to keep his anger in check at that moment led to grievous consequences which will haunt him for the rest of whatever remains of his life.

Jesus Christ our master taught us forgiveness, and we must adopt his admonitions in our everyday lives. Keep your voices low if you must argue. Do it in love if you must quarrel, not forgetting that you are one and can't stay angry at yourselves.

Explain things to one another, ask for forgiveness, forgive, be fair enough to say "I'm sorry" and move on. Remember, you're on the same team. Misunderstandings are meant to make us know each other better and get closer. Importantly, as Ephesians 4:26 preached, we must never let the sun go down on our wrath.

PRAYER POINTS:

- Appreciate the giver of life for the opportunity of a new day.

- Ask for the power to keep anger in check, and to always find peace no matter how perplexed you are.

$\mathcal{D}$ay 3

TABS ON THE MIND

"Whatsoever things are true, ... honest, just, pure, lovely, of good report;
think on these things."
Philippians 4:8

This is a life lesson. The mind is mighty powerful, and is germane in controlling our affairs in reality. Therefore, as Christians, we must always ensure, that our thoughts are positive, and of good desires. The wrong kind of thinking could ruin one's life entirely.

In Proverbs 23:7, the word of God says "For as he thinketh in his heart, so is he". The devil is always lurking around in the shadows, looking for the slightest opportunity and opening to come in and ruin a good thing, and if allowed, he will have his way.

One of the tools he tries to use is the mind, which is why it is important as Christians that we are steadfast and diligent in nurturing and feeding our mind with the word of God to strengthen it against the devices of the devil. When the devil wants to sabotage a marriage, he employs the mind and injects unhealthy thoughts into us. "This marriage isn't going to work" "I should have taken more time" "He or she's cheating on me, his or her familiarity with that woman / man is becoming too pronounced" "It's a good thing we have no children yet, we can still go our separate ways". Thoughts such as these and many others like them are detrimental to any union, if not nipped in the bud in time.

Just as virus spreads in no time, thoughts like these fester very quickly if allowed to linger, and they are devices of hell against your marriage. The marriage has almost a zero chance of survival once these kinds of thoughts are allowed to govern your mind.

It is natural to have fears, and doubts when situations beyond our powers arise, but that is why we are children of God and his promises are for us. God has assured us in his words that his thoughts for us are good and not of evil. Therefore, since God is the foundation of your matrimony, be sure he is dedicated to keeping it together till the end, as long as you don't tear it apart by yourself.

Refrain from entertaining such thoughts that suggest negativity, as they won't get your marriage anywhere than guarantee its end. Our actions are functions of our thoughts, in other words, if the mind is unhealthy, so will the actions be.

Stay clear of anything whatsoever that says differently from what has been established in the scripture and promises of God for his children. Pronounce positivity, and strive to make your marriage work.

Instead of entertaining negative thoughts, approach your fears and doubts with adequate counter actions, be it in form of prayers, or your approach and behavior towards your spouse and marriage.

PRAYER POINTS:

- Give glory to God for a new day and the opportunity to study at his feet.

- Pray and ask for divine victory over an unhealthy mind.

- Pray for divine purification of your thoughts and victory over the devil's attempts at poisoning your mind.

Day 4

THREE IS A PARTY

"Therefore shall a man leave his father and his mother, and shall cleave unto his wife:
and they shall be one flesh."
Genesis 2:24.

As said in this scripture, a married couple is to leave their families, and establish their home.

The scriptures are very straightforward and self-explanatory most of the time, except for cases where one needs special direction by the spirit to interpret what a particular scripture entails.

The above scripture is self-explanatory. Marriage is a covenant between two parties, and should be kept as such. Parents and family are arguably the most important people in anyone's existence, and this scripture says clearly that a man is expected to LEAVE them and CLEAVE to his wife. For the word of God to instruct that you LEAVE your family, which is supposed to be the most important people in one's life, it is clear then, that wedlock is extremely important.

On several instances of break-ups and discord in matrimony, one of the popular reasons are complaints of either of the couple giving way to external influence in running the affairs of the home. A husband must be a man, especially since you are a Christian and a child of the most high, and as such, you are the head of the home. There is no reason whatsoever then, for a head to allow himself be swayed hither and tither by external influence. No wife will feel secure under a husband who isn't a man of his own.

7

A wife on her own is expected to be independent of outside influence. Her husband must be her everything after God. External influence will do nothing but break a home if care is not taken.

As couples, you have one another, and God almighty. Make decisions amongst yourselves, and when things seem beyond your knowledge, you consult the author and finisher of our faith. This however does not mean for you to ignore advices, and counsel from people who are knowledgeable and wealthy in wisdom. No. It is saying, couples shouldn't make it a practice to always involve outsiders in their marriage.

Many homes have been torn apart just because couples neglect the counsel of one another, and exalt the opinions of outsiders. CLEAVE to your spouse, they are your partner, and if you must entertain counsel from outside your home, do so wisely, and make sure to carry your spouse along every step of the way, keeping in mind that the final decision on whatever the case may be must be a consensus between you and your spouse after consulting God.

If this rule is taken seriously, it sure will save a lot of marriages from hitting the rocks.

PRAYER POINTS:

- Bless the heavens for the privilege of witnessing yet another day.

- Ask God for the wisdom, and divine discretion, to handle external influence so that it doesn't bring trouble into your marital paradise.

Day 5

JOIN HANDS IN PRAYER

"Pray, that ye enter not into temptation: the spirit indeed is willing,
but the flesh is weak."
Mathew 26:41.

God said in his words through the scriptures, that where two are gathered in my name, there I am also.

There is no gainsaying, the importance of prayer in Christian life. In fact, it says in the word of God that prayer is the staff of a Christian. In every aspect of our lives, we must consult God in prayer, without ceasing.

It must be rang like a bell into the ears of couples, that they have been joined together for a reason, and made a team to take on greater things, if only they do things right. A married man or woman is not expected to pray only individually anymore, except of course you're praying on behalf of you and your spouse, BECAUSE, there is NO "I" in team. You have become ONE. James 5:16 - "Confess your sins to one another, and pray for one another".

A praying couple builds a healthy home. Here lies the importance of praying twogether as a couple. We must keep reminding ourselves of the fact that we have been made one in Christ, therefore, praying for your spouse means praying for yourself.

- Take your problems to God for solution - TWOGETHER.
- Take your questions to God for answers - TWOGETHER.

- Take your sins and transgressions to God for forgiveness - TWOGETHER.
- Take your weaknesses to God for strength - TWOGETHER.
- Take your ignorance to God for wisdom - TWOGETHER.

We have a guarantee in his word already that he will answer. A Christian who prays receives the grace to go through life with less difficulty, and it looks to onlookers as though it is magic. So also will a praying couple who do it twogether in love will receive grace to push through wedlock with more ease.

Write out prayer points for one another. Create a prayer schedule that will be convenient for both of you. Abide strictly by it, and watch God do unprecedented things in your home.

It must be pointed out, that this admonition is all about the TWOGETHERNESS. You may have been a great prayer warrior as a bachelor or single lady, it is beautiful, but now that you have a partner, how about teaming up and combining your energy and voices to break barriers and do even greater things twogether? Have you considered how far you could go, and how great your results could be when you come twogether as a force in prayer?

Have you given it a thought, that there are requests the heavens won't grant basically because you're asking as an individual instead of as a team? Try it out, the outcome will overwhelm you, and you'll be glad you did.

PRAYER POINTS:

- Appreciate the giver of life for a new day.

- Pray that the almighty God instill in you, the habit to pray *with* one another, at all times.

$\mathcal{D}$ay 6

WHAT GOD HAS JOINED

"What therefore God hath joined twogether, l
et not man put asunder."
Matthew 19:6

S ome years ago, we were on vacation. Due to a storm we were detained on the island of the Bahamas for four additional days. The problem was, we had examinations coming up for our biblical counseling certification, and we had to prepare or we'd fail. Failure was not an option, and so, we did what we had to do. For each additional day we weren't at school to take the exam points were counted against us. We read in the midst of the storm, and went on to pass when the exams eventually. Even though we may not have passed with the score we would have loved to on a good day, we did NOT fail because we were intentional about our study habits.

This is how marriage is.

Life as they say, is not a bed of roses. Marriage is not an exemption. If anyone tells you marriage is a smooth ride, such person lies, but do we because life is not a bed of roses quit or take our own lives? NO.

Therefore, we must keep in mind as Christians, that come what may in our marriage, and no matter what struggles we face, we are sticking twogether, and seeing it through till the end. Divorce is not an option. Not only does it not solve whatever the problem is, the bible also forbids it.

The bible says in Romans 7:2 that "The woman which hath a husband is bound by the law to her husband so long as he liveth." This alone is binding enough to remove thoughts of divorce from our minds as couples no matter what we face. The biblical rule of marriage is that it is an indestructible union.

Your husband will hurt you, so will your wife. They might even betray and fail morally, but that's because they are human, and we fight a constant battle against the flesh. Instead of thinking divorce, why not try forgiveness? Why not take it to God in prayer for fixing? Why not allow God who joined you twogether to do what only he can do, and turn the situation around to his glory?

Marriage is a lifetime commitment, as ordained by God, and thoughts of divorce alone will ruin it. Marriage vows are one of the most solemn and binding duties a person will ever take-on, and it should be protected till the very end. To dissolve it will simply mean to detach one's self from the blessings of God promised in marriage. Whatever it is that threatens the continuity of your matrimony, let GOD FIX it.

PRAYER POINT:

Dear Lord, we thank you for a new day, and counting us worthy to be among the living. Heal our wounds, mend our dents, and fix us completely when and where needed. Remove totally from our hearts, such thoughts as that of dissolving the union you put twogether.

AMEN.

Day 7

MANNER OF SPEECH

"A soft answer turneth away wrath: but grievous words stir up anger."
Proverbs 15:1

Research was done in our grandchildren's school, where children were asked about how their parents communicate with them, and what they liked or didn't like about each manner of communication. We were particularly interested in the study, so we were present at the parents' meeting called after the study's end. The replies were interesting.

A questionnaire was passed in the workplace as ordered from the headquarters and it had a question that was quite similar to that study carried out in our grandchildren's school. The question was asking how our upper management, and co-workers communicate with the employees.

You'll wonder what we're getting at. In the study in our grandchildren's school, the children expressed distaste for being shouted at by their parents or guardians or any adult at all. In the questionnaire at the work place, people expressed distaste too, about co-workers and upper management who always had a harsh tone.

It is not only nice but imperative that we are mindful of our manner of speech at every point towards people. In marriage, love is not to be only professed but acted out and shown. The manner of speech most often than not reflects how we feel towards whoever we are speaking with. Couples must make it a point of duty to speak softly at every point to their spouses.

It has been said in earlier parts that there will always be reasons to be angry, perplexed, on edge, and/or dissatisfied with our spouses. These moments are tests of our love, amongst other things. Never, on any occasion raise your voice at your spouse, or shout at them, or use abusive expressions. These kind of actions are ungodly, and damaging. It is advisable, that when as humans we get angry, we keep mute for as long as it takes for our anger to wear, rather than make regrettable utterances.

Be soft spoken, you kind words, be romantic, be tender and loving. It goes without saying, that speaking in a soft and loving tone reassures your partner of how much you care about them. Loving words melt an angry heart, it calms frayed nerves, it soothes the soul, and re-ignites affection. Harsh words on the other hand do nothing but crash your spouse's desire to please you.

A boss who wants a file looked into in two minutes and approaches his secretary calmly with a warm tone will get results faster than one needs a note corrected in an hour and approaches his secretary harshly.

God is love, and we are his children, therefore we must exude love in all ways. Choose your words and tone wisely. It matters.

Ecclesiastes 9:9 says "Live joyfully with the wife whom thou lovest."

PRAYER POINT:

Thank you father for the grace given to us to study at your feet. Help us to cultivate the habit of speaking lovingly to one another.

AMEN

Day 8

ON MONEY MATTERS

Main Scripture: "It [love] is not possessive... Love has good manners
and does not pursue selfish advantage."
1 Corinthians 13:4, 5.

There are so many aspects of human life, and unavoidably, each aspect has to be re-visited once you start considering getting involved with a partner and getting married, just to make sure to eliminate certain disagreements.

Money is a subject that comes up every time in our daily life. It's importance cannot be overemphasised but it's not curtailed and handled right, money can as well be the downfall of a home.

Firstly, the TEAM concept of marriage: As mentioned before, there is no "I" in team. When you choose to live the rest of your days with a partner and are joined together in matrimony, you become ONE. Therefore, YOUR money, or MY becomes OUR money. Same goes for properties, problems, joy, victories and then some. The subject of money is multifaceted, but we will touch the important ones.

Different couples/families have different ways they operate. In a situation where both couples work and make money, never should there be a battle of supremacy in terms of who earns more or less. There is nothing Godly in that. Bring funds together, make decisions on how to disburse them, stay out of each other's business. For this to work however, accountability is important. As a husband, you must be accountable enough for your wife to trust you not to spend lavishly. The same applies to the wife. This way, both parties trust each other's spending decisions without questioning.

In families where the wife doesn't work. The husband has the obligation to give a certain amount of money (as agreed on by both spouses) for housekeeping (groceries, food items) and her upkeep (cloths, accessories) among other things. This money should be given cheerfully and not grudgingly under protest. "God loveth a cheerful giver." - 2 Corinthians 9:7.

Both spouses must respect that each party retains the right to have certain sums of money at every point to spend without necessarily accounting for. This should not be hard as long as both party lives right in the interest of the union.

A stingy husband may drive his wife to spend lavishly out of anger or spite, just as a lavish one can cause their partner to be stingy. Showing confidence in your companion's managing ability will usually make him or her more businesslike.

If the suggested practice is diligently imbibed, couples may be able to avoid squabbles resulting from monetary disagreements. Conclusively, in the presence of love, which is the greatest commandment, money will not be a problem.

PRAYER POINT:

We thank you Lord for sparing our lives till this day to learn a new lesson from your word. Provide for our monetary needs, and bless us abundantly such that money may not be a problem. Lead us, and teach us how to run monetary affairs prudently, so that it doesn't come between us in Jesus Name

AMEN.

$\mathcal{D}$ay 9

ACCORDING TO GOD

"Love is forbearing and kind. Love knows no jealousy. Love does not brag is not conceited. She is not unmannerly, nor selfish, nor irritable, nor mindful of wrongs. She does not rejoice in injustice, but joyfully sides with the truth. She can overlook faults. She is full of trust, full of hope, full of endurance."
1 Corinthians 13:4-7

It cannot be overemphasized that as Christians, we are a new creature, and a whole different version of ourselves in Christ our savior. This entails a lot of things amongst which is the expectation to forgo whatever it is we have of the world.

There is knowledge, and there is knowledge in Christ. Love as we understood it as ordinary humans is not the same as it is in Christ. A lot of human endeavors fail for the singular reason that we approach them with the confidence of our own knowledge or abilities, and marriage is not an exception. Loving your partner is one thing, understanding what God dictates about love is another.

Many marriages fail today because they are approached based on the knowledge of man. God is love, who better to teach us about it, and how to practice it than God himself?

We are privileged as Christians to know what God teaches on every aspect of life. Therefore, this edge is to be an advantage for us in our journey through life. Wouldn't it be a shame then, if our marriages crumble for the same reasons as that of the rest of the world? Shouldn't we know better?

The word of God is total, and if diligently studied and imbibed, we are sure to scale through life with triumph. Go over the above scripture again, but this time, carefully, with intent to understand in totality each word there-in.

Everything we need to know about love, and how to practice it is right there in this scripture. Imbibe the virtues outlined in there, make them your standard and the benchmark of your relationship. Some of them may not be easy to practice, but with determination, and God's involvement, and a constant reminder that this is it, and that you've signed a lifetime commitment, with time, you will get there.

Nothing done the way God commands can go wrong. Understand his teachings, put them into practice, and watch your home wax strong in the midst of adversities and the many obstacles in the way of a successful marriage.

PRAYER POINT:

Dear Lord, thank you for blessing us with the gift of life and the opportunity to study your word yet again. Grant us the will, and grace, to understand in totality your description of love, and the readiness and dedication to imbibe the virtues.

Help us to grow in love, and commitment to this union you have ordained so much that we become a living testimony and example to our immediate community and the world.

AMEN.

$\mathcal{D}ay$ 10

ZERO CRITICISM

"Why beholdest thou the mote [splinter] that is in thy brother's eye, but considers not the beam [whole board] that is in thine own eye?"
Mathew 7:3.

In a relationship one may not know what to look for in a mate, people are sometimes eager to point out faults in almost everything someone else does. This may cause one to lose their self-esteem and worth.

Criticism is a recurrent problem in relationships these days. Cases of wives complaining about their husbands' habit of criticizing them at every turn, and even in public. It is not exclusive to men. A lot of women also pick faults in their husband's every move.

Don't get me wrong. This is not an attempt at eliminating the presence of faults and shortcomings on the part of either of spouses. Rather, this is an attempt to open our eyes to the fault in the habit of finding faults and criticizing.

Love is all encompassing. As you must have read yesterday in God's description of love. Being in love, and being a Christian does not make you perfect, it only guarantees that you become a better person who is constantly improving in Christ for the person you love.

Instead of criticizing your spouse for their faults and shortcomings, love corrects lovingly. This doesn't only guarantee a change, the change also comes not grudgingly but gladly.

The scripture says in Proverbs 21:19 that "It is better to dwell in the wilderness, than with a contentious and an angry woman."

It is time to quit criticizing and finding faults in your spouse. Understand and embrace the fact that they're just human and entitled to their own imperfections. So, never expect perfection from the flesh. Your spouse may be lacking a few things or attributes, but nagging and criticism won't change anything. Stop trying so hard to change, or force, or reform your spouse. It is not your place. Lessons taught in love are easier imbibed and taken rather than the ones dished out in spite or contempt.

Know that with the right attitude, the right amount of love, cheerfulness, words of encouragement, and prayer, the change you desire in your spouse will come. The power of love and kindness cannot be undermined. Correct your spouse, but do it in love. Nagging and criticism will only dent their self-worth and make them move even farther from change. I will leave you with the word of God in Colossians 3:19 that says "Husbands, love your wives, and be not bitter against them."

If you must correct your partner, do it with love.

PRAYER POINT:

Thank you Lord the giver of life for keeping us till this new day. Give us the divine grace to refrain from nagging, and criticizing each other, and the patience to correct one another with love.

AMEN.

$\mathcal{D}ay$ 11

DON'T LEAVE GOD OUT

"Except the Lord build the house, they labour in vain that build it."
Psalm 127:1

It is not news that tons of Christians tend to forget the place of God when they get too comfortable with what they have or where they are. Some naturally grow into the behavior, some just decide that they don't need him anymore, and some do this out of sheer ignorance or deception by the devil.

We have been admonished in earlier episodes of this devotional according to the word of God to not be ignorant of the devil's devices. One can only succeed and pull through life if God is kept as the center of their existence. He is our creator, the author and finisher of our faith, only in him are we truly safe and secured.

You may have had a fine courtship, and your matrimony may seem to be perfect. None of this is reason to forget or ignore the place that one God who is the foundation and pillar of your union. Carry him along, keep him as your pillar, let him keep ordering your steps, keep learning at his feet, keep doing as he commands, so that you can be guarded against the enemy at every time.

God is not a boy scout, or a fire brigade. You cannot neglect him for long and jump back to him for salvation when trials come, and believe it, trials will come, and they are what makes us stronger in our Christianity.

The word of God has everything we need to know in it. It says in Proverbs 3:6 that "In all thy ways acknowledge him, and he shall direct thy paths.", it says again in Philippians 4:7 that "And the peace of God, which passeth all understanding, shall keep your hearts and minds through Christ Jesus."

What more is there to say? This rule can well be the mother of all others as far as marriage is concerned. Love is important, so is patience, studying the bible, temperance and the rest, but keeping God's place as the center of the union is the greatest key to a continuously happy home. A lot of marriages that suffer disconnection will work if only they allowed God to govern their affairs. It is great fortune to know Christ, and Christians must use this to an advantage.

Have you drifted far from the creator? Have you been operating out of the supposed wealth of your own human knowledge?

Have you taken away God's place in your marriage? Turn back to him today. He is all you need and more. God is love, and with him as the center of your union. YOU WILL NOT FAIL. Trials will come, the enemy will try, but you will not stumble.

PRAYER POINT:

Dear Jesus, we give you thanks for sparing our lives till this beautiful day. Grant us the wisdom to know your place and your importance in our home and Christian life, so that we will never make the mistake of pushing you aside.

AMEN.

$\mathcal{D}$ay 12

RESPECT HER/HIS RIGHTS

"Love is forbearing... Love knows no jealousy. ... She is not unmannerly, nor selfish. ...
She does not rejoice in injustice. ... She is full of trust."
1 Corinthians 13:4-7

This is a subject that comes under many headings, today, we will attempt touching the very important ones.

PRIVACY:

There is no debating the fact that everyone has a right to their privacy. This right should not in any way be trampled on or undermined by anyone. However, people's likeness for their privacy varies. Some people prefer to be in other's companies, while some won't trade their privacy for anything.

It is true that marriage makes you one, and therefore demands that you live not as a single entity but as a team, but, this does not take away the fact that both parties have their personal space.

You may not use the same purse. You may not use one toothbrush. You may not wear the same lingerie, amongst many other things. In other words, each person is entitled to their personal space and privacy. Spouses should not try to invade this privacy, or crowd their partners' space. Don't sniff around your partner's bags, don't go through their phones, and don't search their closets except on permission. It is a show of insecurity to do these things, and if it eats deep into the fiber of the union, trust issues spring from insecurity.

MISGIVINGS:

Don't take away the fact that your spouse is human, and each of us reserve the right to our misgivings and wrong doings. When this happens, make sure not to make too much of a fuss about it. Point out their fault lovingly, keeping in mind that you will do wrong too sometimes and wouldn't want to be given havoc for it. Romans 12:10 - "Be kindly affectionate one to another with brotherly love; in honour preferring one another."

SOLITUDE:

Every once in a while, we feel the need to be left alone, just to think, relax or meditate among other things. This need for solitude must not be questioned whatsoever. There is no disputing the chance in cases where one partner prefers the company of their spouse, and the other likes the occasional alone-time that there may be grumbling and distaste on one hand, but couples need to remind themselves that marriage partners don't own each other, and so they must never try to impose change on each other as the outcome may not be pretty.

Instead of trying to alter your spouse's ways, and imposing yourself on their space, concentrate on loving them right, and pleasing them. This may actually help him effecting the change you desire in them.

Our homes will be better for it if these things are noted and imbibed. It works like clockwork.

PRAYER POINTS:

- Appreciate God for life and another chance to learn more from his words.

- Ask for the tolerance and discretion to know and respect one another's privacies and privileges without nagging.

Day 13

DUTIFULNESS AND ORDERLINESS

"She works with willing hands." "She rises while it is yet night and provides food for her household." "She looks well to the ways of her household, and does not eat the bread of idleness."
Proverbs 31:13, 15, 27.

Finding a good spouse is one thing, keeping them is another. One either has the characteristics and traits that keeps a home functioning, or one doesn't, there are no two ways about it.

It is important for us to cover all grounds in order to make our marriage work. In other words, half righteousness isn't enough.

You are Godly, very beautiful. You're spirit-filled, prayerful, loving, and tolerant. All these are good traits too, but they are not enough. All grounds must be covered. We bless the Lord for the word he has given to us, and the completeness of the teachings there-in. The bible is complete, we can't stress this enough.

The beauty of a home is orderliness. A wife is expected to have a number of virtues, and orderliness is one. We will agree that there are certain things that aren't just the husband's responsibility, except of course, if he decides to assist his wife with them out of love - which is important to do every once in a while (we will talk about this in subsequent days). A wife's ability to keep the house in good shape and order accrues her a pass mark and a special place in the heart of her husband.

Shortcomings like dirtiness, and laziness are so grievous that they may not be overlooked. Husbands are naturally rugged, and less concerned about orderliness in the home with the exception of a few who are meticulous, and most times, the wife brings that order husband lack. What then will be the value of a wife who isn't orderly and dutiful?

Keep your house in order at all times, and your husband will be proud of you and forever bless the day he met you. Husbands must however make it a point of duty to lend helping hands in keeping this order in their own little way when they have the opportunity to do so. An orderly and clean home is aesthetic, and has a kind of serenity and peaceful atmosphere that it establishes, making the home conducive for all parties involved. "Let all things be done decently and in order." – 1 Corinthians 14:40.

Make delightful meals, and more importantly, make them ready on time. Feeding your husband constantly, and timely does a great deal in impressing on his heart. He naturally will be pleased with you at all times for taking good care of him. Wives know this.

Imbibe these traits, and watch them improve your marriage drastically. It works.

PRAYER POINTS:

- Glorify God for his mercies, and his magnanimity for granting your life and the privilege to be part of a new day.

- Pray for the zeal and motivation to be dutiful and orderly in the home. Husbands should join their wives in making this request too.

$\mathcal{D}$ay 14

THE ROLE OF A PROVIDER

"If any provide not... for those of his own house, he hath denied the faith,
and is worse than an infidel."
1 Timothy 5:8.

Yesterday's message was mostly directed at the wife, so, it is only fair that today addresses husbands. You may take this as a lesson in its own; Fairness to each other no matter the odds.

As commanded and ordained by God, the man is the head of the home. This title comes with tons of responsibilities. Responsibilities that must not be fallen short of, especially since each man has the support of their helper - the wife. As the head of the family, a husband is the sole provider. For purpose of clarity, the word "Sole" can be translated to mean "Major". This means, there is room for seeking assistance, but that must be after the husband has performed his responsibilities to a great extent.

It is not alien to anyone, that there are husbands who don't see the need to be responsible, and thus fail to provide for their homes. As Christian husbands who have been fed with the word of God, we must not find any one amongst us who fails at their duty of providing for their home.

Just as a wife needs to be dutiful and orderly in her overseeing of the affairs of the home, so must a husband be agile, up and doing, hard-working, and committed to making sure that he caters for the home which he governs. God has given you all you need to be a real man, and all you need do is rise up to the challenge and approach your duties in earnest.

Quit sitting around complaining and mumbling. Your creator - God has provided what you will need to feed on and sustain your home, but it will not be delivered at your door step, he just needs you to work, and show a genuine sense of responsibility before letting it all fall on your laps.

Proverbs 6: 6-11 "Go to the ant, O sluggard; consider her ways, and be wise. Without having any chief, officer, or ruler, she prepares her bread in summer and gathers her food in harvest. How long will you lie there, O sluggard? When will you arise from your sleep? A little sleep, a little slumber, a little folding of the hands to rest,..."

It is a disgrace to manhood, and an insult to our almighty God for a husband to be lazy and fail in providing for his home. The scripture is our watch word, and it says in the book of 2 Thessalonians 3:10 that "For even when we were with you, this we commanded you, that if any would not work, neither should he eat". God disapproves of laziness, and if he is our pillar, we will not do what he disapproves of.

His commandment is that the husband is industrious and work to feed his family. "Be ye not slothful" is what Hebrews 6:12 preaches.

So, husbands, while your wife toils dutifully to put the home in order, go out and work, so that she will not go hungry.

PRAYER POINT

Lord Jesus, we thank you for this new day and the lesson you've taught us. Bless the work of my hands so much so that I can be the man you want me to be, and provide for my home.

AMEN.

(Wives can join in on this prayer for their husbands).

Day 15

COUNSEL TOGETHER

"Seest thou a man wise in his own conceit? There is more hope of a fool than of him."
Proverbs 26:12.

We were collected and reserved people. We prefer being on our own, and doing things ourselves without troubling other people. Whenever we felt the need to ask questions from someone, we turned to one another. Being private and reserved you miss great opportunities to witness to other married couples who may need assistance. With time, seeing married couples Sunday after Sunday needing something we were able to give made us take a look at ourselves, we both have the gifts of giving, mercy and serving. Therefore, we can offer a married couple something which God gifted to us.

Remembering when we were in one of our certification programs sharing notes and text books, discussing topics that proved difficult and many other things, we naturally opened up and became quite free with our course mates. So, when we had tests, we looked over our notes together after reading, trying to ask questions and see how prepared we were. We did assignments, term papers, and projects together. It was hard to not counsel with my course mates, especially since we were studying the same course, our aims were the same - success.

We used the analogy above to explain why it is important in marriage to seek each other's counsel.

Is there any need to stress the fact that once you're married, you cannot live or do things like you were still single. You have become a team, and your spouse your partner, with a common goal.

Therefore, at every point in time, you both are to carry each other along, and counsel with each other. This should be an important tool in decision making between couples. Every issue concerns you both, from taking a job offer, to purchasing a car, to acquiring a property, to disbursing funds and so on. This said, both spouses are to deliberate on everything and reach a consensus before making moves, so as to promote together and avoid supremacy or grudge. No-one is to singlehandedly make decisions on anything without consulting with the other person.

Talking things over together will avoid many blunders that could ruin your marriage. You are a team, and should each of you behave like a team mate.

However, on occasions where a consensus isn't reached between couples, the bible has just the right word for you on what to resolve to in Ephesians 5: 22-24 22 "Wives, submit yourselves unto your own husbands, as unto the Lord. 23 For the husband is the head of the wife, even as Christ is the head of the church: and he is the saviour of the body. 24 Therefore as the church is subject unto Christ, so let the wives be to their ...".

In other words when a unified conclusion cannot be reached, the wife is to submit to her husband's decision.

PRAYER POINTS:

- Appreciate God for the new day and the abundance of opportunities it presents.

- Ask for the humility to always consult with your spouse before making decisions.

$\mathcal{D}ay$ 16

STAY TRUE TO ONE ANOTHER

Wherefore putting away lying, speak every man truth with his neighbor:
for we are members of one another.
Ephesians 4:25

Lying is bad. There is no debate about this. The damages it does are so grievous they may never be repairable. We are familiar with the attributes of lying, and how one has to keep telling other lies to cover up the ones from the past. There is only one way to it, and that is to never do it, because once it's done, there's no coming back, except of course one decides to come out and speak the truth. This is always very tough. Several relationships have been severed singlehandedly by lying, including marriages.

Christians have the word of God as a guideline for living our lives. God detests liars. It says in Proverbs 6, verses 16 through 19 that God hates 7 things, two of them are lying and deceit. It should not be found in the life of a Christian.

ABOUT MARRIAGE:

Marriage is a union between two people, where they come together to become one, and team mates on the same side with common goals, aspirations and objectives. Is there any further need to stress the importance of straightforwardness and truthfulness to your spouses?

How does a team progress if the team mates are not on the same page? How does a team achieve their goal, if the parties on the team are not truthful with one another? Failure is guaranteed in a marriage where honesty is absent. It breeds insecurity, trust issues, and eventually whatsoever love was in the marriage will gradually fade.

Quick question: If we take the bible as our guide and watchword, perfectly understanding the teachings there-in, how are we ever going to be comfortable being dishonest to anyone, let alone our life partners?

If we know beyond doubts that lying is a sinful act that God disapproves of, how can we bring ourselves to exhibit it towards someone whom this same God has commanded us to love and cherish forever?

The foundation of marriage is Christ, and your union should be built on this foundation, and trust. Not a one-sided trust, but mutual trust. So, when you begin to tell lies and deceive your spouse for whatever reasons, you are not only gradually destroying the foundation of your union, you are also committing a sin against God.

Situations may arise sometimes, where lying appears to be the easiest way of solving, but keep in mind, that the aftermath is never pleasant, and once trust is broken, it is almost impossible to rebuild.

Conclusively, be truthful to your spouse in all ways, speak the truth no matter how hard it may seem, and never make promises you will not keep.

PRAYER POINT:

Dear Jesus, we thank you for the new day, and for sparing our lives to see it. Grant us victory over lying and deceit, so that we will live according to your words, maintaining the foundation of our union.

AMEN.

Day 17

CONTROLLED SPENDING

Love not the world, neither the things that are in the world. If any man love the world, the love of the father is not in him. • For all that is in the world, the lust of the flesh, and the lust of the eyes, and the pride of life, is not of the Father, but is of the world. • And the world passeth away, and the lust thereof: but he that doeth the will of God abideth forever.
1 John 2:15

Earlier on, we touched mildly on money matters, and how couples should trust one another to act appropriately when it comes to spending. It was stressed, that each person is entitled to their own personal money and spending decisions which must not be questioned.

Today, we are talking about spending as regards to the team (family). Spending must be controlled. There's no better way to say it than that. Uncontrolled spending equals waste of scarce resources, and resultant debts. We as a Christian home should know better than coveting what other people have, or trying to match up to other people's standards. It has come to light that most of the time, the reason families run into debts is that they spend lavishly on things they don't actually need, and cannot afford. Then there comes the back and forth about who's to settle the debts and how.

The home should be the priority, and not material things. Money is to be spent wisely and prudently, on the basic necessities to make life easier. People try so hard to keep up with the society and lose sight of what is truly important. Why work long hours on a job, just to make enough money to enjoy material luxury, while you gradually miss out on the chance to spend quality time with your family, and neglect your duties towards the church?

Married couples need to strategize and find a way around their spending. Adopt whichever method will work for you. Make a budget, and adhere strictly by it. Draw a list of the important things you need against the available cash. If in the end, it looks like you won't have enough. Money left for the upkeep of the home, and to contribute to God's work, revisit the list, and adjust it until it is right.

Desist from making debts you won't be able to pay. Avoid unnecessary debts. You are eliminating a huge bottleneck when you do this. Guard your expenses, it is for the good of your home.

PRAYER POINTS:

- Appreciate God for the gift of life, and the privilege to witness a new day.

- Pray for the discretion to differentiate what's important from what is not, and the contentment to be happy in your home with what the Lord has given you.

Day 18

HUSBANDS, RULE WITH LOVE

Likewise, ye husbands, dwell with them according to knowledge, giving honour unto the wife, as unto the weaker vessel, and as being heirs together of the grace of life; that your prayers be not hindered.
1Peter 3:7 -

A wise man once said, if there is love, power wouldn't be of any value. He must have said this after a critical evaluation. The statement is quite true if you look at it. If love reigns, things will be done willingly and lovingly without need for much persuasion, let alone force. Since no-one will be asking of another, things that are almost impossible or too difficult. Power and force are exerted to impose or force another person to do something they normally will not.

God is love, and as our master, we must strive to be just like him, and act according to his teachings.

Marriage is a union between two people, ordained by God, and just as the scripture pronounced the man as the head of the family, commanding wives to submit to and obey their husbands, it also commands that the man who is the head, must lead lovingly.

It is not strange news that majority of husbands misuse and abuse their position as the head of the home, and that many marriages have been dissolved from this attitude. As Christians anyway, we are not of the world, and must do things differently. Husbands, not at any point should you abuse your role or position as the head.

Your wife is your partner. Seeing her as a subordinate may be the genesis of your marital troubles. Without knowing, you will become a villain, and sooner or later, she will get to her elastic limit and turn on you. Wives aren't slaves, or a material possession. They are to be treated with respect as valued companions.

Don't let your manly ego ruin you. Don't exploit your authority by using it to get your own way every time. Don't make decisions on your own without consulting your wife to arrive at a unanimous conclusion in the best interest of the team. Be a team player. This however does not mean as a husband you shouldn't exercise your position when the need arises. All you need is direction, and the discretion to act accordingly as each case demands.

Lastly, to err is human. Your wife may misbehave, or disrespect you on occasion. It is with love that you must handle such situations. Do not exercise power. Let love lead. If we do this, we cement our union more in Christ.

PRAYER POINTS:

- Appreciate God for the new day and the privilege he's given you to be a part of it.

- Pray twogether that the almighty take total control of the heart of the head of the home.

- Ask that the Lord quenches the urge to exploit your position, or exert force, and plants in you the attribute of leading with love.

$\mathcal{D}ay$ *19*

SEXUAL PURITY

Proverbs 5: 1-18.

For purpose of space, we may not outline the bible passage here. You will read this out loud from your bible. However, reference will be made to relevant verses as we proceed.

It is agreeable, that infidelity may well be in the front row of reasons why marriages crash. We will have failed woefully at teaching couples about this were we to shy away from it in this book.

Marriage is a huge step in life. It is to be thought through thoroughly, and taken on without any doubt in the hearts of both partners whatsoever. That said, given that we are Christians, and have God as the center of our existence, we will resolve that your marriage was ordained by God.

God disapproves of divorce or separation of married couples. It is his commandment that under no circumstance should it be considered *except* on one occasion. The occasion of course is adultery. A marriage can be dissolved as long as either of the couple defiles the marital "bed" by laying with another person. This point is raised in an attempt to show the gravity of adultery, and the weight of its consequences.

Marriage is the only ordained relationship for satisfying the need for a lifetime partner, and for sexual desires. Anything outside of this is against God's blueprint.

Never should any of the couples allow themselves to flirt, or lust, or covet, or desire anyone other than their ordained partner. Mark 7: 20-21:

"And he said, that which cometh out of the man that defileth the man. For from within, out of the heart of men, proceed evil thoughts, adulteries, fornication, murders."

Therefore, remove yourself from thoughts such that can lead you to defile your home. We cannot over emphasize the ill adultery does to relationships and matrimony.

First, as the matrimonial bed is defiled, it gives opening for bitterness and hatred (Prob. 5:4). There is no gainsaying the difficulty a marriage faces to survive once hatred sets in.

Secondly, according to the bible passage, disrespect, distrust, and grief creep into the home.

Thirdly, and quite important, a destruction of the flesh and body, in other words, the risk of venereal and sexually transmitted diseases.

HOW TO CONQUER:

Not taking the fact that we are yet humans and susceptible to temptations, it is suggested, that we must individually identify our weaknesses, and avoid them as much as we pray for victory over them.

Revive your sexual relationship with your partner if it's dwindling already. Make your sexual relationship sweet, lively, and satisfying. Please one another, and try new things. This will help a long way in guarding against promiscuity.

PRAYER POINTS:

- Give thanks to God for granting you the opportunity to study and learn at his feet as a team.

- Appreciate him for keeping your home twogether to this point, and his plans to keep you twogether even forever.

- Ask that he gives you victory of the flesh and it's lustful yearnings, that you may not fall into a temptation that could ruin your home.

$\mathcal{D}$ay 20

EXPRESS YOUR SEXUALITY

"Nevertheless, to avoid fornication, let every man have his own wife, and let every woman have her own husband. - Let the husband render unto the wife due benevolence: and likewise also the wife unto the husband. - The wife hath not power of her own body, but the husband: and likewise also the husband hath not power of his own body, but the wife. - Defraud ye not one the other, except it be with consent for a time, that ye may give yourselves to fasting and prayer; and come together again, that Satan tempt you not for your inconsistency"
1 Corinthians 7: 2-5

Praise God.

Take a moment to appreciate God for his holy book before you continue reading. The bible covers every ground, with answers and solutions to every question and problem respectively.

Yesterday, the focus was on sexual purity and fighting the temptation to defile the matrimonial 'bed'. So, it is only appropriate that today we talk about the one thing that can safeguard us against such temptations.

Sex is an expression of love. Let us erase the word 'Sex', and adopt 'Love making' instead. Love making is an expression of love, and in marriage, you have an obligation to satisfy each other's sexual desires. You have been ordained to be together forever, therefore, you have only one another to engage in such activities with. You might as well make the best of it.

Be expressive: You are nude before your partner. You belong to them as they belong to you. Therefore, remove any barriers of expression. You are not to be shy or reluctant around each other. Ask what you want, express your desires and cravings, and in love, because you are committed to pleasing one another, your partner will please you.

Keep the fire burning: Many couples resign to a certain routine after marriage. This takes away the spice and sparkle of the relationship. Try out new things in the bedroom. Don't be stereotypical. Explore each other's fantasies. Take each other's breaths away. Flirt with your spouse. It revives the fire, and it works wonders.

Read the bible passage above again carefully. It is stated that never is either of a couple expected to deprive the other of sexual pleasure. Except when they are both abstaining for purposes such as fasting and praying, after which they both must come together again. Sexual denial and starvation opens door for temptation, and the result may not be palatable.

Conclusively, Revive your sexual relationship with your spouse. Spice it up. Don't hold back. Continuous practice of this brings about a deep connection between couples, what more, with time, you get to understand each other's body languages better, and discover how best to satisfy and please one another in bed. Get to work now, and keep temptation at bay.

PRAYER POINTS:

- Thank the most high God for the gift of life, and a new lesson the day brings.

- Ask for everything you think you will need to activate a fulfilling sexual relationship with your partner. AMEN.

$\mathcal{D}$ay 21

BE APPRECIATIVE

Render therefore to all their dues: tribute to whom tribute is due; custom to whom custom; fear to whom fear; honour to whom honour.
Romans 13:7 -

This is the biblical teaching to all Christians generally, as to be applied in their doings. Give honor to whom it is due.

This topic is so interesting. You'll see why. Our God is a God who feeds basically on praises. In our Christian journey, we must have been taught or have found out on our own how much God enjoys praise and thanksgiving. When we praise God, it is like urging him to embarrass us with even more blessings. A man of God once said in a sermon that he doesn't ask God for anything anymore. All he does is just thank him for the ones he has done, and praise him in advance for the ones yet to come. That is our God. He loves praises. Give him praise, and he'll surprise you with blessings.

If our God has laid down this principle of "Praise and receive more", who are we then to not observe and practice it amongst ourselves? Especially in matrimony. Praises and appreciation are instrumental in affirming value and encouraging both continuation and improvement.

HUSBANDS:

Proverbs 31: 28, 30-31 - "Her children arise up, and call her blessed; her husband also, and he PRAISETH her. Favor is deceitful, and beauty is vain: but a woman that feareth the Lord, she shall be praised. Give her of the fruit of her hands; and let her own works praise her in the gates.

As a husband, it is one of your duties to show appreciation to your wife, and exalt her from time to time, to remind her that you know how fortunate you are to have been blessed with such a virtuous wife. Wives do not get paid for their many troubles of keeping the home in order and supporting their husbands. So, the least you can do is to show genuine appreciation from time to time. In words, actions, presents, and whichever other way you deem fit. This does not only make her fulfilled and respected, it gives her a sense of value and worth. Start today, and you'll be glad you did.

WIVES:

Ephesians 5:33 - "Nevertheless, let every one of you in particular so love his wife even as himself; and the wife see that she reverence her husband".

Being the head of a house and the sole provider is a serious job. There is no way you can pay your husband back for this great service. He settles the bills, spends time with you and the kids, creates a beautiful atmosphere for his family to blossom, never lags in his duty to you as a wife, and many more things. A show of appreciation and an acknowledgement that he is doing a good job at being a husband could be all he needs. Appreciate your husbands, let them know their impact is felt. Do this, and watch him be an even better man than he already is.

PRAYER POINTS:

- Thank the almighty for his mercies, and the privilege he's given you to see this day.

- Ask that he cultivates in you a habit of appreciation and praising your spouse so that they are charged to willingly keep up the good work.

$\mathcal{D}ay$ 22

CONFLICT MANAGEMENT

For the woman which hath an husband is bound by the law to her husband so long as he liveth; but if the husband be dead, she is loosed from the law of her husband.
Romans 7: 2

The scripture above is applicable to both parties.

What better scripture to admonish ourselves on this topic than the one above?. You ask why? It is simple. The reason is because this bible verse tells us about God's command and stand point on the permanence of the marriage union.

This rule is what must be kept in mind by both parties in the face of conflict or misunderstandings, no matter how big, or complicated. "We are ordained and bound by God's law to be twogether FOREVER, therefore, this conflict MUST be resolved".

We have talked about this earlier in this book, but this time, we are looking at means to resolve conflict. Understand first, that conflicts will come. It is only natural. How we handle it when it comes however, is what matters. It is what determines if we will grow strong and learn from the conflict, or if it will ruin our union. Needless to say, it is better to choose the former.

Couples must come twogether and identify their problems, talk about them, device ways to resolve them, and put the plans into action. Bear in mind that you are a formidable force in Christ, and no conflict should have victory over you.

TURN TO GOD:

"Be careful for nothing; but in everything by prayer and supplication with thanksgiving let your requests be made known to God. And the peace of God, which passeth all understanding, shall keep your hearts and minds through Christ Jesus." - Philippians 4: 6, 7.

Usually in the midst of life's troubles, we get overwhelmed so much that we lose all hope. It is advisable, that before things deteriorate that much, we must acknowledge the almighty God and go to God in prayer for intervention. Only God can turn a hopeless situation around, and only to him shall we run when we find ourselves in such situation.

TRUST AND OBEY HIS WORDS

"Trust in the Lord with all thine heart, and lean not unto thine own understanding. In all thy ways, acknowledge him, and he shall direct thy paths". - Proverbs 3: 5, 6.

It is our habit as humans to try and govern our affairs on our own. When marriages develop problems, most couples turn to shrinks, therapists, counselors, and psychologists for advice and solution. This most times doesn't work, basically because the solutions and advices received from such sources are not found in Christ but human wisdom. Why not search the scripture and study what it says and teaches about your problems, and watch how God helps you to use what you have learnt in mending your problem.

The list goes on, but conclusively, take this into cognizance, search God's heart in the scripture, understand his teachings, obey them, put them into action, and you'll be better for it.

PRAYER POINTS:

- Appreciate God for the new day, and the lesson there-in.

- Ask for divine guidance and direction to handle conflicts appropriately so that you come out strong.

Day 23

SELFLESSNESS & SELF SACRIFICE

*"Husbands love your wives, even as Christ
who loved the church and gave himself for it"*
Ephesians 5:25 -

First and foremost. It must be established, that the passage above applies to both husband and wife.

The word of God is complete. We cannot say this enough. It has everything you will ever need. It holds answers to all questions. If only we will study it dutifully and pray for understanding.

Jesus Christ our Lord and Savior came as human and laid down examples in practice for all Christians to follow as regards all aspects of life. His greatest lesson is love, and there is no greater example of self-giving and self-sacrifice.

In marriage, as we have established that two has become one, and as such are a team that should do everything hand in hand for the betterment of the team and achievement of common goals, it is therefore needless to say, that each partner must be selfless. They must stop thinking for/about themselves as an individual. Every once in a while, situations arise that test our love. We will fail these tests if our love is not true.

Self-giving is an attribute of love, and it mustn't be lacking in our relationships. Couples should always be willing to happily go out of their ways to please their partners, or for the sake of their union. Most times, work, and/or businesses could be what we need to adjust and reschedule just so we can meet with the emotional needs of our spouses and family. We mustn't hesitate in doing so.

This also extends to character changes. There are certain behaviors and habits that we may have developed as individuals over the years - behaviors that don't sit well with our partners. Habits are of course hard to drop, but that's where self-sacrifice comes in. We must be willing to work on ourselves in adjusting and eventually dropping such behaviors/habits.

In events of misunderstandings and quarrels too, it helps most times when a partner is always ready to assume the fault and blame even when they aren't the one at fault, and saying sorry regardless, just so that peace will reign. This may be called 'Taking one for the team'. Waiting for the other person to say sorry or admit a fault. You aren't in a contest. Do what you must to make sure peace reigns at all times.

Also, there are desires. Each individual has desires/wants/interests. Occasionally there may be a conflict of these things. Or rather, the pursuit of these things may not in the long run benefit both parties as a team. Be ready to let go of such desires without grudge or malice. You will be saving your marriage a lot of unnecessary squabble.

On a passing note, be self-giving, and be always willing to take one for the team without hesitation. You are one, and will remain one forever.

PRAYER POINTS:

- Bless God for the abundance of his grace on your lives, and his magnanimity in sparing your lives till this day.

- Ask him to teach you, and plant in you the spirit to willingly sacrifice for the good of the team.

Day 24

FORGIVENESS: BURY THE HATCHET

Take heed to yourselves: If thy brother trespass against thee, rebuke him; and if he repent, forgive him. And if he trespass against thee seven times in a day, and seven times in a day turn again to thee, saying, I repent; thou shalt forgive him.
Luke 17: 3-4

Jesus knew how hard this virtue is to imbibe and put into practice, that's why he made such a thorough ruling about it. To explain how important an attribute it is in the life of a Christian.

It says in the Lord's prayer Mathew 6: 12, 14, 15 - "Forgive us our trespasses 'As We Forgive Those Who Trespass Against Us'.". The latter part of that prayer is a clause. It is the prerequisite for the first part. Meaning, if we expect forgiveness from the father for our sins, we must first forgive those who have sinned against us. We will agree, that we all have reasons to ask for God's forgiveness countless times daily, and if God refuses to forgive us each time we ask, just because our sins are grievous or we sin too often, we may be in a lot of trouble.

In marriage, your partner will hurt you. It is expected as they are not perfect. As God teaches, we must forgive them each time. This also means that whoever is in the wrong mustn't hesitate to take responsibility and atone for their sins.

The tricky part of forgiveness though is letting go. Many of us say or think we forgive our brethren and partners, whereas we never truly let go of their transgressions. Most of us are even tempted to always bring up previous trespasses just to hurt or spite our partners. This is not a healthy behavior. They have apologized for it, let it go, look past it, focus on the present and future, those are the important things.

Question: Would you like the Lord to remind you of your previous sins every once in a while just to let you know he's not forgotten? I guess not.

It may be very hard to forget wrong doings, but it is unacceptable reminding your partner that you have not forgotten. Instead, work on flushing the memories of past transgressions out of your consciousness so you can move past it.

Conclusively, let us take a lesson from the Indians. The ancient Indians cultivated a habit in their time. Whenever there was conflict between tribes and it was resolved, they came twogether and made peace, agreeing to symbolize the peace pact by burying a hatchet. This signified that, even though everyone knows where the hatchets were buried, no-one will go and uproot them to hurt another.

Forgiveness should be total.

PRAYER POINTS:

- Show gratitude in your own words for the grace given unto you to be among the living today.

- Ask him for forgiveness of your sins, both individually, against one another, and as a team against God.

- Ask that he teaches you how to totally forgive one another, and move past it once and for all.

Day 25

SERVICE TO GOD: THE MAIN GOAL

"For I know him, that he will command his children and his household after him, and they shall keep the way of the Lord, to do justice and judgments; that the Lord may bring upon Abraham that which he hath spoken of him.
Genesis 18:19.

If a student whose dream is to be a computer scientist gains admission into college to study computer science, the main goal is to study and get the degree. However, there is room for picking and gathering other important knowledge from here and there in the course of his study, because no knowledge is lost, and together, these knowledge can make them a better person. BUT, never at any point must the student lose focus or forget why they're in school.

The passage we read earlier speaks of Abraham and how he orders his house. Husbands are the Abrahams of their homes, and are expected to order their homes accordingly. Lessons can be taken from Abraham (read more about him).

The major goal and objective we must work towards twogether as a home is serving God, and making heaven. To avoid misconception and misinterpretation however, this is not saying families must not pursue other important goals like establishing love, building a healthy relationship, raising God fearing children, and pursuing comfortability amongst other things. No. Just as in the example made in the first paragraph.

The message here is that no matter what we do, or chase, our sights must not be removed from the major goal, because all other achievements become void if service to God is not given priority. Make it a point of duty for your family to be right with God in all things.

Put it in practice to praise him both individually, and collectively. Study his word twogether as a unit, where questions are raised, explanations are given, and each member of the family is admonished to live by the teachings in the word.

Assign a service to God to each member of the family. You can make yourself useful to the Lord in any capacity. Either by supporting the church and it's growth, praying for the church and the servants, spreading the word of God through evangelism which may be done verbally, or by distribution of tracts and so on.

Instill in each member of the family the habit of supporting one another in prayer. Not forgetting however the importance of praying as a unit.

In summary, ensure that your family lives to please the Lord. Let this be your focal point. Make God the first and the blessings of Abraham can be yours too.

PRAYER POINTS:

- Give glory to the father for keeping you till this day for a chance to hear from his heart again.

- Pray that the heaven gives you all you may need to diligently seek to live your life as a family to the glory of God at all times..

Day 26

ACCOUNTABILITY:
LET YOUR WORDS MATCH ACTIONS

"My dear children, let us not love in word, neither in tongue;
but indeed and in truth"
1 John 3:18.

"I Love You"

"You're priceless"

"I Cherish You"

These things are very nice to say, as are several other sweet expressions. Need I say, that saying them seems to always be the easy part. The important part, which is the hard part is letting your actions match and correlate with the things you say to your partner.

The world today is filled with lies. People forging their ways to where they want to be or get what they want basically by false pretense, exaggerations, lies and the likes. They say "Whatever it takes to achieve what you want".

We are children of God and are not of the world. Therefore, behaviors, or characters such as these mustn't be found in us. People lie and feign affection just to get attention and probably win the heart of another person. We will agree however, that this home wasn't founded on false professions of love and affection.

As the Lord admonished in the bible passage above, expressions of love to your partners must not be only verbal. Yes, you are to say it in words how you feel about one another, but be sure that your actions confirm and not negate what you confess.

You love your wife? Do you pray for her? Do you lend helping hands when you can? Do you satisfy her sexual desires? Do you encourage/uplift her when she's down? Do you pamper her like a baby? Do you try giving her a massage when her bones are weak from plenty work? Do you buy her gifts to appreciate her efforts? Do you make her breakfast when you have the time on weekends? Do you consider her in your decision making? Do you respect her?. Answer these questions honestly. If you don't do these things, how then is she to believe you when you say "I love you"?. Or, which other way do you show love to her?

You cherish your husband? Are your actions convincing enough for him to brag about your love for him? Do you support him in prayer? Do you assist financially when you can? Do you help boost his confidence every now and then? Do you please him in the bedroom? Are you submissive enough? Do you accord him the respect he deserves? Ask yourself these questions. If you're failing in any of them and more, how then do you show him the love you profess?

A lot of homes have lost the fire and sparkle, just because couples fail to match their words with actions. In the long run, the words entirely lose their meanings when spoken.

Match your words with appropriate actions, and see how your relationship blossoms.

PRAYER POINTS:

- Thank God for the gift of life

- Thank him for keeping your home twogether so far.

- Appreciate him for the privilege to study his word.

- Ask for the grace to do as you say, and not opposite.

$\mathcal{D}$ay 27

TOGETHERNESS & QUALITY TIME:

Fulfil ye my joy, that ye be like minded, having the same love,
being of one accord, of one mind.
Philippians 2:2

This is what the bible teaches. Twogetherness ranks high among the attributes and characteristics of couples. You both have been joined TWOGETHER, and should pursue every means to remain so.

Most often than not, we get busy attending to the various duties and responsibilities life throws our way, and it is therefore very easy to forget, or be removed from fulfilling our responsibilities towards our partners. Especially when most of the time we can say "After all, all I'm doing is so I can give my family a good life". Understand that there is nothing wrong in being responsible and striving to do right by your family, but who says you have to do it alone and bear the burden all by yourself?. Is this not why you have a partner to do things twogether with?

Make sure to not be swallowed by responsibilities so much that you're too detached from the family you're trying to provide for. Twogetherness is a major key to establishing and maintaining happiness in the home. Have family moments. Observe stay-home days, when everything is attended to as a family unit.

QUALITY TIME:

It is not right to hear a married man or woman complain of loneliness. It is also a huge failure when couples cannot boast of knowing each other well. Practice they say makes perfect. By spending time with one another, uninterrupted and undistracted by the outside world, you learn more about one another. You understand each other better, and improve in ways to deal, and handle each other.

You will never get to know certain things about your partner except you spend quality time with them, and this ignorance will wait to mess things up for you much later. Knowledge of our partners is like a password or remote, because per time, you can be sure of what they want or don't want, and you can easily decide how to please, placate, pamper, spoil, and surprise them whenever you wish.

The excuse people have mostly is that they are busy with work. Truly, one can be busy, but the fact remains that we will always have time for the things that are important to us. Organize your time, and make sure you dedicate a considerable part of it to being with your spouse. If you had time to spend with them during courtship, marriage should not be any different.

Spend time twogether. Don't be eager to leave one another. Play twogether. Talk about everything. Let love grow and wax strong over the years. It is to your advantage, because it is a disaster, to become strangers to a spouse you live with under the same roof just because you fail to spend time with them.

PRAYER POINTS:

- Appreciate God for the blessing of a new day, a new opportunity, and a new lesson.

- Ask him to teach you how to best maximize time, so as to have enough for the important things.

$\mathcal{D}$ay 28

PROMISES

If a man vow unto the Lord, or swear an oath to bind his soul with a bond; he shall not break his word, he shall do according to all that proceedeth out of his mouth.
-- Read the chapter further. It speaks about the woman too.
Numbers 30:2

Promises breed a lot of things. Among them are hope, expectation, and confidence. All of these stated offspring's of promises and more are that can result to devastation if the promise that bred them is failed. It is therefore important to be careful about making promises so as not to raise false hope, expectations or confidence, and to also make sure to be committed to fulfilling promises once made.

Marriage is an oath. It is kicked off with pronunciations of oaths and promises. Promises that MUST not be failed under any circumstances. It is believed, that before deciding to take the step and walk down the aisle, both parties must've individually made up their minds with all certainty that they want to spend the rest of their lives with the other person. There shouldn't be any problem therefore with keeping the promise they make at the altar. Many times, from the various cases of marital problems we hear, it is evident that couples have somewhat forgotten all about their oaths and promises towards their partner and to the sacred union. Take this as a reminder. Marriage is not a casual relationship. It is binding. It is a commitment.

PROMISES IN MARRIAGE:

The bible says blessed is the servant that applied wisdom. It is agreed that promises are to be made after deep thinking and must be kept. So, while couples are admonished to please be careful about empty promises and raising false hope in their partners, we must also point out that in event that a partner fails to come through with a promise, the other person should be understanding enough to not make a fuss out of it, or allow it become a serious problem between them.

Firstly, you are a team, and are to remain so forever, so, if a promise is failed today due to certain circumstances, be sure that a lot more will still be made and fulfilled if Christ tarry.

Secondly, understand that there are circumstances under which a person can be relieved of their promises. The bible makes allowance for this. Read Mathew 18: 24-34, Luke 7: 41 and 42. Since you know your partner will not make a promise they aren't going to keep, be willing to relieve them of promises when unexpected circumstances come up.

Altogether, couples; do not make empty promises to one another. Remember your marriage vows, and keep them. Be willing to relieve one another of promises when things don't work as planned.

PRAYER POINTS:

- Dear Jesus, we thank you for sparing our lives till this new day, and for strengthening our union with your word and teachings.

- Strengthen us to keep our vows and promises, and grant us divine understanding and discretion to recognize when to relieve one another of promises. Amen.

$\mathcal{D}ay$ 29

RAISING GODLY CHILDREN

Train up a child in the way he should go: and when he is old,
he will not depart from it
Proverbs. 22:6.

It would be a very inappropriate oversight to not talk about this. It is the desire, and obligation of every marriage to produce offspring's. The bible commands it in Genesis 9:7 - 'And you, be ye faithful, and multiply; bring forth abundantly in the earth, and multiply there-in.

Bringing children into the world is not where it ends, couples are to know that these children are their responsibilities. You brought them to the world, and therefore the onus is on you to shape them to be the best children they can be. The glory of God must be obvious in the lives of your wards, and it is important to state, that your kids are a reflection of your lifestyle.

Secondly, the bible says children are God's heritage. They are a gift from God, and he has given them to you to be custodians. Need I say that God holds you responsible for these kids and what becomes of them?. You certainly don't want to fail God. This said, as a team, certain things are expected of you.

LAYING EXAMPLES:

Children are very sensitive. Nothing misses their notice. Parents are the first role models of children, and so, they watch our every move and try to emulate us. We must strive in all ways to set good and Godly examples for them. Failure to do this will only result in them exhibiting the same bad behaviors they copy from us or whoever it is they watch.

CO-OPERATION

As a team, we must be on the same page when it comes to training our children. It will not lead anywhere profitable if we have conflicting and irreconcilable ideas and systems of raising our children. In fact, we indirectly preach objection and separation by not being on the same page in our approach of training them.

TIME:

No parent should be too busy to dedicate quality time for their children. If you leave your children unattended, in the end, the riches you try to gather may amount to nothing. Both parties must pay keen attention to their children. Monitor their growth and progress. Be a part of their growth. If possible, don't miss anything.

Couples must not abandon duties when it comes to their children. A father/husband has his place and responsibilities, likewise the mother/wife. Husbands shouldn't leave their duties to the wives. Likewise, wives shouldn't leave theirs to their husbands.

Conclusively: Counsel them. Direct them. Teach them. Pray for and with them. Your children are your responsibilities. Handle them with utmost dedication and commitment. God will hold you responsible for the results you get.

PRAYER POINTS:

- Appreciate God for life, the new day, and the children with which he has blessed you. Or that you're sure he will bless you with (If you're yet to have).

- Ask for direction on how to raise your children to become what God wants them to be, and the grace to excel as parents.

$\mathcal{D}$ay 30

BE TEMPERATE IN ALL THINGS

And every man that striveth for the mastery is temperate in all things. Now, they do it to obtain corruptible crown, but we, an incorruptible.
1 Corinthians: 9:25

For further readings see 1Corinthians 10:31.

Moderation is the watch word here. Just as inadequacy is bad, too much of anything (excessiveness) isn't good either. It will take a lot of discretion and God's guidance however to know the appropriate amount or extent to which to do things.

Overdoing things usually ruin whatever good work we may have put into it. In marriage, couples need to be careful to not overdo anything. Be it work, play, affection, sex or anything else. Everything must be done moderately and balanced up. If you overdo work, you become too weakened in mind and spirit to be present or attentive to your spouse. If you overdo affection or love, you end up being overbearingly annoying and crowding your partner's space. Be moderate in all your doings. If you overdo sex, you exhaust each other and eventually exhaust the pleasure and intrigue it has. It also weakens you spiritually. There are times when the need arises to take a breather from sex. We have to understand that as sex is important between couples, marriage doesn't give license for excessive sexual activities.

As much as it is required of couples to be contented with the counsel of one another, and avoid external influence, it is good to socialize every once in a while, especially since the friends you're expected to keep are children of God also. Boredom will creep in if couples live in isolation from the rest of the world.

It is expected of Christian families to engage in service to the church, however, overdoing this so that the home begins to lack adequate attention and commitment doesn't look too good. In training children also, you must be firm and strict, but this should be done moderately too. Children are sensitive, and excessive enforcement of discipline could cause them to stray or dread us. Therefore, as you instill discipline, be liberal enough to allow them to make their own mistakes and learn from them.

A little bit of everything is to be employed to spice up your lives. Do things with discretion. Know when to stop, when to slow down, when to adjust, and when to intensify as the case may be. This is not a call to be perfect or superhuman. It is to help to work at making ourselves the best versions of us for our spouses.

On a passing note, do not allow overzealousness, or intemperance to destroy your marriage. Make moderation your watch word.

PRAYER POINTS:

- Give thanks for the gift of life and of a new lesson.

- Appreciate him for how far he has brought you as a family, and how further he's willing to take you.

- Ask God for the spirit of temperance, and that he order your steps towards moderation in everything you do. Amen.

MEET THE ROUSSAWS

MEET HIM:

Minister Dwight is the founder of Husbands United®, a husband's ministry offering husband's coaching, husband's mentoring, annual husband's conferences, husband retreats, monthly husband's bible study and hosts a monthly husbands prayer call. Minister Dwight is a passionate speaker, he affectionately has a jubilant and unique teaching style, which involves using his God given capabilities.

Hidden secrets in a marriage or relationship becomes a spreading disease as cancer dispenses throughout the body, if detected sooner rather than later your marriage can be healed with the calling of help from the second to none surgeon Jesus who is the Christ!

Minister Dwight's humbleness and dedication draws husbands to become Godly leaders in their marriage.

~ His Husband Verse ~

"Live joyfully with the wife whom thou lovest all the days of the life of thy vanity, which he hath given thee under the sun, all the days of thy vanity: for that is thy portion in this life, and in thy labour which thou takest under the sun" ~ Ecclesiastes 9:9

MEET HER:

Minister Deidra is the founder of TrulyWed Wives®, a wives ministry offering wife coaching, wife mentoring, wives retreats & an annual wives conference, wives night out, savvy wife tool box - Prayer, finance, communication, infidelity, inspiration, blended family, healing, investments, marriage counseling, intimacy, couples devotion, weight management assistance, wellness, image consultation, romance concierge and date night.

Minister Deidra is an author of a book she compiled with 31 other wives titled "Wives on Fire!"

Minister Deidra is currently enrolled in the Success Mastery Coaching Class under the leadership of Dr. Stacia and Arianna Pierce.

Minister Deidra hosts a weekly radio show, she serves as the romance coach for TrulyWed Wives offering pleasurable resources and romantic exposure for couples to partake in for the purpose of strengthening and enhancing their marriages. Minister Deidra is committed to provide exuberant experiences that will invoke passion and devotion to the sanctity of marriage.

~ Her Wife Verse ~
"A wife of noble character is her husband's crown" ~Proverbs 12:4

MEET THEM:

Mr. and Mrs. Dwight Roussaw, married August 8, 1998 exemplify the portrait of a Christ-centered and Christian-based marriage. They are the proud parents of one daughter and the loving grandparents of four grandchildren and (a grand angel).

Dwight and Deidra responded to God's call to participate in a marriage ministry in 2004. They began their journey by serving in leadership roles which included an Assistant Vice-President position for the Sharon Baptist Church Marriage Ministry in Philadelphia, Pa. under the leadership of Bishop Keith W. Reed Sr. Dwight & Deidra are currently serving as Ministers of Marriage and are servant leaders for 2 Be One Marriage Fellowship which is located at The Resurrection Center in Wilmington, Delaware under the leadership of Bishop S. Todd Sr, Ph. D. & Pastor Cleo V. Townsend, Ph. D.

Mr. and Mrs. Roussaw value and credit their mentors, Pastor Emanuel Sr. and Lady Martina Lambert for their instrumental role in sharing their knowledge and experience and in providing effective training and guidance.

Both Dwight and Deidra are Certified Marriage and Relationship Coaches through World Coaching Institute and International Coaching Science Research Foundation. They are Certified Marriage Mentors through The Marriage Academy and they studied biblical counseling at:

- The Christian Research & Development;
- PAIRS Foundation (Redefining Relationships),

and are currently certified instructors for Family Dynamics Institute, teaching the "Dynamic Marriage" seminar to married and engaged couples. Dwight and Deidra are also members of the Beyond Affairs Network, Kingdom Chamber of Commerce, National Association for Relationship and Marriage Education's (NARME) and Toast Masters International.

This dynamic duo husband and wife team are the founders of TWOgether Marriages®, a marriage ministry that offers personalized coaching and mentoring programs. Additional programs fostering healthy relationships will include successful dating protocols and they are the hosts of the annual Marriage on FIRE Retreat and Marriage Sailabration.

Dwight and Deidra are passionate about their vision of providing a faith-based ministry; applying God's principles for marriage and offering both dating and married couples a biblical framework and platform for a spiritual and healthy relationship.

Dwight & Deidra are also the owners of Kairi's Travel®, which is a full service travel agency consisting of over 12 trained, certified and experienced travel consultants. They have been serving the travel industry since 1997. Their calling is Christian "group" & "couple" escorted tours. Both are experts in Caribbean and Cruise travel. Their expertise is priceless and their services are complimentary. They are destination wedding specialists, certified Sandals & Beaches WeddingMoons Specialists, Disney College of Knowledge graduates and members of CTO (Caribbean Tour Organization) and CLIA (Cruise Line International Associates).

~ Their Marriage Verse ~
"Come aside by yourselves to a deserted place and rest a while!"
~ Mark 6:31

NOTES

www.ingramcontent.com/pod-product-compliance
Lightning Source LLC
Chambersburg PA
CBHW032027040426
42448CB00006B/753